IF FOUND, PLEASE RETURN TO:

NAME _____

ADDRESS _____

_____

PHONE _____

E-MAIL _____

ONE
SKETCH
A DAY

A VISUAL JOURNAL

CHRONICLE BOOKS
SAN FRANCISCO

ISBN 978-1-4521-8456-2

Manufactured in China.

Cover art by SpaceFrog Designs.
Design by Kayla Ferriera.
See the complete One Sketch a Day series
at www.chroniclebooks.com

10 9 8 7 6 5 4 3 2 1

Chronicle Books LLC
680 Second Street
San Francisco, CA 94107
www.chroniclebooks.com

A YEARLONG RECORD OF SKETCHES—

because every daily drawing is worthy of remembrance.

HOW TO USE THIS SKETCHBOOK

Each page has space for two days of sketching. To begin, enter today's and tomorrow's dates at the top and bottom entries of the first page. Now, just sharpen your pencil or take out your pen and let the creative juices flow. You might find inspiration in your everyday surroundings, or you can let your imagination run wild! However you fill these pages, they will become a document of your creative journey over a year.

DAY 1   DATE _____

DAY 2   DATE _____

DAY 3   DATE _____

_____

DAY 4   DATE _____

DAY 5   DATE _____

DAY 6   DATE _____

DATE _____

DATE _____

DATE _____

DATE _____

DAY 11

DATE _____

DAY 12

DATE _____

DAY 13   DATE _____

DAY 14   DATE _____

DAY 15   DATE _____

_____

DAY 16   DATE _____

DAY 17   DATE _____

_____

DAY 18   DATE _____

DATE _____

DATE _____

DAY 23

DATE _____

DAY 24

DATE _____

DATE _____

DATE _____

DAY 29   DATE _____

DAY 30   DATE _____

DAY 31

DATE _____

DAY 32

DATE _____

DAY 33

DAY 34

DATE _____

DATE _____

DAY 39

DATE _____

DAY 40

DATE _____

DATE _____

DATE _____

DAY 43

DATE _____

DAY 44

DATE _____

DATE _____

DATE _____

DAY 47

DATE _____

DAY 48

DATE _____

DATE _____

DATE _____

DAY 51

DATE _____

DAY 52

DATE _____

DAY 53

DAY 54

DAY 55   DATE _____

DAY 56   DATE _____

DATE _____

DATE _____

DATE _____

DATE _____

DAY 63

DAY 64

DAY 65

DATE _____

DAY 66

DATE _____

DATE _____

DATE _____

DAY 71

DATE _____

DAY 72

DATE _____

DAY 75

DATE _____

DAY 76

DATE _____

DATE _____

DATE _____

DATE _____

DATE _____

DATE _____

DATE _____

DAY 89   DATE _____

DAY 90   DATE _____

DATE _____

DATE _____

DAY 93

DATE _____

DAY 94

DATE _____

DAY 99

DATE _____

DAY 100

DATE _____

DAY 101   DATE _____

DAY 102   DATE _____

DAY 103

DATE _____

DAY 104

DATE _____

DATE _____

DATE _____

DATE _____

DATE _____

DAY 111

DATE _____

DAY 112

DATE _____

DATE _____

DATE _____

DATE _____

DATE _____

DAY 119

DATE _____

DAY 120

DATE _____

DAY 123   DATE _____

DAY 124   DATE _____

DATE _____

DATE _____

DAY 127

DATE _____

DAY 128

DATE _____

DAY 133

DATE _____

DAY 134

DATE _____

DAY 136

DAY 139   DATE _____

_____

DAY 140   DATE _____

DATE _____

DATE _____

DAY 145

DAY 146

DAY 147

DATE _____

DAY 148

DATE _____

DAY 149

DATE _____

DAY 150

DATE _____

DATE _____

DATE _____

DAY 157   DATE _____

DAY 158   DATE _____

DATE _____

DATE _____

DAY 165

DAY 166

DAY 167

DATE _____

DAY 168

DATE _____

DATE _____

DATE _____

DAY 179

DATE _____

DAY 180

DATE _____

DATE _____

DATE _____

DATE _____

DATE _____

DAY 189

DAY 190

DATE _____

DATE _____

DATE _____

DATE _____

DATE _____

DATE _____

DATE _____

DATE _____

DAY 203   DATE _____

DAY 204   DATE _____

DATE _____

DATE _____

DAY 207

DATE _____

DAY 208

DATE _____

DATE _____

DATE _____

DAY 215

DATE _____

DAY 216

DATE _____

DATE _____

DATE _____

DAY 223

DATE _____

DAY 224

DATE _____

DATE _____

DATE _____

DAY 227   DATE _____

DAY 228   DATE _____

DATE _____

DATE _____

DAY 235   DATE _____

DAY 236   DATE _____

DAY 243   DATE _____

DAY 244   DATE _____

DAY 251

DATE _____

DAY 252

DATE _____

DATE _____

DATE _____

DATE _____

DATE _____

DAY 259

DATE _____

DAY 260

DATE _____

DATE _____

DATE _____

DAY 263

DATE _____

DAY 264

DATE _____

DATE _____

DATE _____

DAY 271

DAY 272

DATE _____

DATE _____

DATE _____

DATE _____

DAY 281   DATE _____

DAY 282   DATE _____

DATE _____

DATE _____

DAY 287

DAY 288

DATE _____

DATE _____

DATE _____

DATE _____

DATE _____

DATE _____

DAY 300

DATE _____

DATE _____

DATE _____

DATE _____

DATE _____

DATE _____

DATE _____

DATE _____

DAY 320

DAY 321   DATE _____

DAY 322   DATE _____

DATE _____

DATE _____

DAY 329   DATE _____

_____

DAY 330   DATE _____

DAY 331

DATE _____

DAY 332

DATE _____

DAY 333   DATE _____

_____

DAY 334   DATE _____

DATE _____

DATE _____

DAY 340

DATE _____

DATE _____

DATE _____

DATE _____

DATE _____

DATE _____

DAY 347   DATE _____

DAY 348   DATE _____

DAY 349

DATE _____

DAY 350

DATE _____

DATE _____

DATE _____

DAY 357   DATE _____

DAY 358   DATE _____

DATE _____

DATE _____

DATE _____

DATE _____

DAY 365

DAY 366

CONGRATULATIONS!

You made one sketch a day for a year.
What will you do next?

FACES TO REMEMBER

ARTISTS TO REMEMBER